AN EMOTIONAL MENAGERIE

An A to Z of poems
about feelings

An Emotional Menagerie

Emotions are like animals:
No two are quite the same.
Some are gentle; others, fierce;
And some are hard to tame.

Inside this book there's twenty-six
Emotions you might feel.
Arranged alphabetically
From Anger on to Zeal.

Each poem is a rhyming guide
To different ways of dealing
With whichever emotion you
Might happen to be feeling.

They're full of new words to expand
Your vocabulary,
Helping you develop your
Emotional literacy.

Mastering emotions is
A very useful skill.
With it, you'll grow up to be
More calm, wise and fulfilled.

So open up and come inside
As we set out to see
The weird and wild emotions in
This verse menagerie.

A is for Anger

If Anger was an animal,
It would have teeth and claws,
A mangy mane, a bristly tail,
And growling, gaping jaws.

It comes along when things go wrong,
When our plans go awry.
When toys are broken, trainers lost,
Or favourite treats denied.

It bares its teeth and starts to roar:
'Unkind!' *'Unjust!'* *'UNFAIR!'*
It wants the world to be just so,
Without problems or cares.

To let it go, remember this:
Life won't always go right.
Some things we'd like to happen won't;
Some things we wouldn't, might.

It's sad, we know, and that's the point:
In fact, that's why we rage.
Anger is sadness in disguise:
Our hurt let loose, uncaged.

Life lets us down now and again:
You, me, and everyone.
So next time Anger rears its head,
Accept this, and move on.

B is for Boredom

If Boredom was an animal,
It would have jellied skin,
Limp tentacles, a boneless head,
And a deadening sting.

It washes up when tasks or days
Feel like they'll never end:
Car journeys, homework, shop queues, chores,
And wet autumn weekends.

It lies there like a burst balloon,
Flat, hissing out complaints:
'Are we there yet?' 'Am I done?'
'I'm so bored I might faint.'

It stings us all occasionally.
(Yes, grown-ups get bored too!)
Sometimes we must just wait until
The tedious part is through.

But don't forget to listen, too:
For Boredom's just a clue
That shows us what we don't like doing
And what we'd rather do.

To wash it back into the sea,
Listen to all it says,
And try next time to spend your time
In more exciting ways...

C is for Curiosity

If Curiosity was an animal,
It would have a jet-black beak,
Beady eyes, coal-coloured wings,
And scrawny, scratching feet.

It loves to peck at mysteries:
Those things it doesn't know.
It wants to find the answers so
Its own knowledge might grow.

It makes us feel inquisitive
To understand things more:
'How do planes fly?' 'Why is grass green?'
Or 'what are earlobes for?'

We're fascinated by new things,
The secrets of the Earth.
We get engrossed in facts and dates,
And prize them for their worth.

The best people are curious:
The smartest and most fun.
They know that learning's valuable,
And learning's never done.

You should feed your Curiosity
By finding out more stuff.
For all the world is interesting
If you look close enough.

D is for Daydreaming

If Daydreaming was an animal,
It would live in the trees,
Staring out at land and sky,
Forgetting what it sees.

It slouches in those moments when
We let our minds just wander,
And lose track of the time as we
Invent, imagine, ponder.

We might say we are lost in thought;
Perhaps we're miles away.
We're letting idle fancies free
To wander where they may.

Some grown-ups don't like Daydreaming;
They'd rather we were working.
They think it's a distraction from
Important tasks we're shirking.

But Daydreaming's a kind of work:
It helps us clear our brains
So thoughts we've as yet just half-thought,
Can now make themselves plain.

Try to daydream once a day
And see what comes to mind.
Perhaps write down the thoughts that come
And see what you can find.

E is for Embarrassment

If Embarrassment was an animal,
It would have a coat of spines,
And when it feels it's being watched
It grows to twice the size.

It gets puffed up when we're on show,
And we feel too exposed:
Maybe we've called our teacher 'Mum',
Or spilt food on our clothes.

It makes us feel humiliated
By stupid things we do,
Or mortified that people stare
And sometimes giggle too.

Others seem so self-assured,
So confident and cool,
Whereas we're awkward, somewhat odd:
A stumbling, bumbling fool.

But here's the truth: so's everyone.
We all are fools at heart.
We just don't know each other's thoughts;
Can't spot the foolish parts.

To deflate our Embarrassment
We should laugh at our flaws,
Own up to all our weaknesses
And greet them with guffaws.

F is for Fear

If Fear was an animal,
It would have four skittish feet,
Two pricked-up ears, one twitching tail,
And rather large front teeth.

It burrows in when danger strikes,
Or when we feel it's near.
When lights go out, strange noises sound,
And our fate feels unclear.

We might say we feel anxious
About what might take place,
Or nervous that we might be hurt,
Or ruined, or disgraced.

The world can be a scary place.
And since we're only small,
It's natural to be fearful of
Dangers that might befall.

But sometimes Fear grows far too big
And burrows in too deep.
It stops us from enjoying life:
We feel sick and lose sleep.

The best way to get rid of Fear
Is to tell someone we trust.
For everyone gets scared sometimes;
Sharing helps us adjust.

G is for Guilt

If Guilt was an animal,
It would have hangdog eyes,
Drooping ears, slow-dragging paws,
And a voice that whines and sighs.

It hangs its head when we've done wrong,
And feel it deep inside.
When we've stolen, broken rules,
Cheated, hurt or lied.

It makes us feel deeply ashamed
About the things we've done,
Or culpable for all the pain
We've caused friends and loved ones.

It's useful to feel Guilt sometimes;
It helps us to be good:
Avoid the things we shouldn't do,
Prefer the ones we should.

Though too much Guilt is less ideal
When it becomes self-hate.
We should remember kindness too:
Forgive our own mistakes.

We all mess up from time to time
(It's part of who we are).
Guilt goes some way to mending us,
But kindness goes as far.

H is for Happiness

If Happiness was an animal,
It would have golden wings,
And all the world would thrill to hear
The joyful song it sings.

It visits us on pleasant days:
Flies down from high above
When we are praised, or spoilt, or hugged;
When we feel safe and loved.

We listen to its merry tune,
The melody it plays.
Then look again to find, alas!
It's somehow flown away.

Happiness is a flighty thing,
It comes and then it goes.
One minute it's perched in our lives,
The next it's... well, who knows?

We'd like to catch it in a cage
So it might stay for good.
But it can't help but fly when faced
With some less pleasant mood.

Appreciate it whilst it's here,
And don't mind when it's gone.
Someday it will alight again
To fill our hearts with song.

I is for Insecurity

If Insecurity was an animal,
It would wear a plastic cone,
Avoiding other animals
So they don't laugh, or groan.

It starts when there's some part of us
That we've grown to dislike:
When we don't like our hair, or clothes,
Or weight, or skin, or height.

You could say you're unconfident
Or that you're feeling meek.
Where once you felt bold, now you're shy;
Where once felt strong, now weak.

Our self-worth's often changeable;
It shifts from day to day.
It's easy to let doubt creep in
And worry have its day.

And yet our worth in other's eyes
Tends to be much more stable.
Our friends remember our true worth,
Even when we're unable.

To shed our Insecurity,
Hold tight to the above.
See yourself through friendly eyes;
Remember you are loved.

J is for Jealousy

If Jealousy was an animal,
It would have emerald scales,
A coiled body, a darting tongue,
And a twitching, pointed tail.

It slithers by when others have
Things we want for ourselves:
Fancy shoes, the latest phone,
Or praise for doing well.

It leaves us feeling covetous
For things we don't possess,
And envious that friends or foes
Seem so unfairly blessed.

Jealousy's an ugly beast,
And a common one at that.
It's natural to look at ourselves
And yearn for what we lack.

For Jealousy points out for us
Our own deepest desires:
Those hidden wants and secret dreams,
Which stoke our jealous fires.

Note down what you feel jealous of
And use this as a guide
To plan the life you'd like to lead,
The path you hope to find.

K is for Kindness

If Kindness was an animal,
It would bumble, bob and buzz,
Pollinating living things
With goodwill as it does.

It buzzes by when our eyes spy
A person who's in need
And wish to give a remedy
Of kindly words or deeds.

We might call it benevolence,
Altruism, compassion:
To treat our fellow creatures in
A kindly, loving fashion.

Kindness springs from empathy,
Which means to recognise
How we'd feel if we saw the world
Through someone else's eyes.

How hard we'd find it, being them,
With all their discontents.
How much we might appreciate
A hug, or compliment.

Kindness runs in short supply
(At least compared with hate).
So spread it when and where you can,
To help it germinate.

L is for Loneliness

If Loneliness was an animal,
It would glide throughout the deep:
No ears to hear its lonely song,
No company to keep.

It starts to moan when we're alone,
And sometimes when we're not.
In groups where we're not understood
And feel like afterthoughts.

We feel rejected, overlooked,
Unnoticed and unseen,
As though some broken part of us
Keeps us from fitting in.

Most people never know us well;
They see our surface only.
They never glimpse our hidden depths,
So leave us feeling lonely.

We're only ever fully known
By an elected few:
Perhaps our siblings, or best friends
(The closest one or two).

They know our quirks, our faults, our dreams:
The things that make us *us*.
So seeking out their company
Can soothe our Loneliness.

M is for Melancholy

If Melancholy was an animal,
It would wallow in mires,
Mulling over woes and cares,
And situations dire.

It's similar to feeling sad,
But also not the same.
It's sadness mixed with wise pity;
Sadness without blame.

We call such moments bittersweet:
They're bitter since they sting;
Yet sweet because we recognise
They're common to all things.

Life is just plain sad in parts:
Hearts are quick to break;
Friendships end; people are cruel;
We all get sick, and ache.

We're not in mourning for ourselves,
But rather all of life.
It's our wise reaction to
A universe of strife.

When life seems cruel, just think of how
It's cruel for everybody.
Remember this to turn sadness
Into wise Melancholy.

N is for Naughtiness

If Naughtiness was an animal,
It would gibber and shout,
Making faces, throwing food,
And monkeying about.

It swings in and makes its din
When we're hemmed in by rules:
'Tuck your shirt in!' 'Eat all your greens!'
'You can't wear *that* to school!'

We call it being mischievous
Or disobedient:
The desire to misbehave
And be recalcitrant.

It's good to break the rules sometimes:
A dose of Naughtiness
Stops us getting too solemn,
Uptight and serious.

But when it involves being cruel,
Or straining others' nerves,
It ceases to be wise or fun,
And feels most undeserved.

So make sure, when this mood next strikes,
You think of the effects.
Will you show up pompous fools?
Or hurt those you respect?

O is for Obsession

If Obsession was an animal,
It would build endless dams,
Beavering away all day
To create more logjams.

It gnaws when we get hung up on
A person or idea:
Perhaps a boy or girl we like;
A hobby we hold dear.

We're fixated; preoccupied;
Our minds become possessed.
We think of nothing but this thing
By which we are obsessed.

The more we dwell on this object,
The less we deal in facts.
We fabricate and speculate
And covet what we lack.

It's hurtful when these plans and schemes
Prove to be fantasies,
Foundering upon the rocks
Of cold reality.

Obsessions can be painful then,
But also useful too:
They show us our deepest desires
Even if they don't come true.

P is for Panic

If Panic was an animal,
It would just run amok,
Getting into quite the flap,
Emitting squawks and clucks.

It startles when our problems seem
Far too complex to solve.
We're under pressure, but we're stuck
And so lose our resolve.

We might say that we've lost our nerve
Or that we're freaking out,
Imagining catastrophes
We're sure will come about.

But when the going seems too tough,
We shouldn't lose our heads,
But rather think deeply about
Reality instead.

If things go wrong, the world won't end,
The sky itself won't fall,
And whilst there may be obstacles,
We'll find ways through them all.

If the worst came to the worst
We'd find a way to cope:
You're more resilient than you think
And in this truth, there's hope.

Q is for Quarrelsomeness

If Quarrelsomeness was an animal,
It would have curling horns
And use them to charge straight into
The targets of its scorn:

Sisters who mess up our rooms,
Brothers who muck around,
Classmates who make cruel remarks,
Parents who let us down.

It's sometimes called belligerent
Or argumentative:
We're in the mood to shout, not speak;
To squabble, not forgive.

A fight is a failed debate,
A talk that's run off course.
We can't explain ourselves in words
And so resort to force.

We're scared of being vulnerable,
Admitting we've been hurt.
And instead use insults (or fists)
To parry and divert.

Rather than quarrel, why not try
Explaining how you feel?
An honest statement of your pain
Can help your wounds to heal.

R is for Remorse

If Remorse was an animal,
It would have a wrinkled trunk,
A furrowed, worried forehead,
And a heart forever sunk.

It comes when we think of the past
And wish to make amends.
How we might do things differently
Had we the time again.

We feel regret at our misdeeds,
Repentant and contrite.
Remembering bad things we've done
Can keep us up at night.

Yet no one lives a perfect life.
We all make some mistakes,
So shouldn't dwell too long on all
The paths we didn't take.

Our errors cannot be unmade
But can be overcome,
If they're seen not as tragedies
But things we can learn from.

Contained in moments of Remorse
Are lessons we should heed.
They might not be the kind we like
But could be those we need.

S is for Shyness

If Shyness was an animal,
It would drag around its shell,
So when it feels out of its depth
It has somewhere to dwell.

It tries to hide, or climb inside,
When people that we meet
Seem strange or unfamiliar
And too daunting to greet.

You can call it timidity,
Or sometimes bashfulness:
We worry that our minds are too
Mismatched to truly mesh.

We take an outward difference
(Like age, or sex, or race)
And blow it up until it seems
Too crucial to displace.

Yet, though we're different outwardly,
We're all alike within.
The same excitements, hopes and fears
Lurk beneath every skin.

To swap Shyness for confidence
Remember this is true:
Underneath, all strangers are
As shy and scared as you.

T is for Tranquillity

If Tranquillity was an animal,
It would stand still and graze,
Fixing the horizon with
A steady, placid gaze.

It's also called serenity,
Or feeling we're at peace:
Those moments when our minds just clear
And all our worries cease.

Such moments seldom come about:
Our lives are too fast-paced;
We rarely give ourselves the right
Amount of thinking space.

Some surroundings can make us calm:
A misty field at dawn;
A snowy garden, late at night;
A fireside that's warm.

It also helps if we let go
Of all our nagging thoughts:
The bad things we should not have done,
The homework that we ought.

To be more tranquil, focus on
The pleasant here and now:
The smell of grass; the sound of birds;
The cool wind on your brow...

U is for Uncertainty

If Uncertainty was an animal,
It would keep changing colour,
From red to green, to black, then blue,
Then bright yellow, then duller.

It changes hues when we're confused
And can't make up our minds.
We're being asked to make a choice
And yet we can't decide.

We might say we're ambivalent,
Or feel vague, or unsure:
We're being tasked with nothing less
Than seeing the future.

We make decisions based on what
We glean or guess might happen,
Hoping that events unfold
According to this pattern.

But the future's an uncertain place
Whose shape we can't control.
So full of possibilities,
We can't predict them all.

Rather than chasing certainty,
We should make peace with doubt,
And trust that we'll make the best of
Whatever comes about.

V is for Vulnerability

If Vulnerability was an animal,
It would be red with spots,
And small in size – easily squashed
By anything that's not.

It beetles in when we have been
Upset or hurt of late.
A bruising blow has left us in
A fragile, weakened state.

We might say we feel sensitive,
Or perhaps delicate.
We're leaving our defences down
And our hearts opened up.

Though sticks and stones may break our bones,
Cruel words can hurt far more.
It can take years to recover
From emotional sores.

Some grown-ups tell us, 'Suck it up.'
'Be brave and you'll prevail.'
Not seeing that the braver thing
Is to admit we're frail.

It's no shame to be vulnerable.
In fact, you should take pride:
It's concrete proof that you possess
A caring soul inside.

W is for Worry

If Worry was an animal,
It would be ever wary,
With one eye always watching for
Predators large and scary.

We tend to Worry about things
(Like dentists, or exams)
We can't prevent, where the control
Lies outside of our hands.

When Worry hangs around too long
It's called anxiety:
Which means to Worry all the time,
Without pause, constantly.

Whilst Worry tends to ebb and flow,
Anxiety hangs on,
Filling our every moment with
Its brand of vile poison.

It therefore pays to prune worries
Before they grow too big:
To cut them down to their true size;
Keep them in perspective.

To nip your worries in the bud,
You should say them out loud,
And, in so doing, realise how
Survivable they sound.

X is for eXcitement

If Excitement was an animal,
It would never sit still:
Leaping, bleating, gambolling,
For the sheer blooming thrill.

It frolics when we're fired up
By what the future holds:
Parties, presents, ice cream, cake,
Delights yet to unfold.

We might say we feel stirred, or roused,
Or impassioned, or thrilled.
We're bursting with the prospect of
Our hopes being fulfilled.

Whilst most excitements come and go,
There are some that stick around:
Those we call our passions; those
That feel the most profound.

It's these that show us how to live
And give us reasons why.
They point out goals and targets we
Should set our compass by.

So make a list of excitements
That make you most content,
And turn them into projects for
A life of fulfilment.

Y is for Yearning

If Yearning was an animal,
It would drift on the tide,
Forever lost in longing for
A joy it's been denied.

To yearn means to desire what
We know we'll never own:
A gadget we can ill afford;
A pretty face we've known.

We dote and pine and crave and ache
For this beloved thing,
Whilst knowing, in our heart of hearts,
It won't be ours to cling.

For Yearning is a fact of life:
To live is to desire.
In every human heart there burns
Some unrequited fire.

The best form of consolation
For those who're doomed to long
Is creation: to transform pain
Into a poem, or song.

So don't keep Yearning fruitlessly;
Make use of your bruised heart.
Take its ever-ignited flame,
And turn it into art.

Z is for Zeal

If Zeal was an animal,
It would work tirelessly:
Collecting leaves and insects to
Support its colony.

We tend to feel most zealous when
A job, or task, or act
Feels meaningful – almost as though
It wasn't work, in fact.

We say we are engrossed, engaged,
Highly motivated.
We feel like we could strive like this
Until we're old, or dead.

The acts that feel most meaningful
Are those that we maintain
Will increase others' happiness
Or decrease others' pain.

Humans are social animals:
They live to help their kind.
To buy or make or achieve things
That bring them peace of mind.

To find an outlet for your Zeal,
Think about others' needs
And how you might find novel ways
To meet them with your deeds.

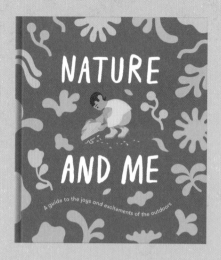

Nature and Me

A guide to the joys and excitements of the outdoors

An essential guide to encourage children to explore, enjoy and benefit from the natural world around them.

Children are constantly being told how important nature is and that natural things are good for them. But it's still often hard for them to know why nature might actually be fun, uplifting, consoling – and a real friend for them.

This is a book about how nature can touch us all and help us with our lives (especially when we might be feeling bored, sad or lonely). We learn about the ways in which we can come to love and be inspired by various examples of nature, like:

* a giant anteater
* a view of the Alps
* a flatfish
* the night sky
* an okapi
* a cuddle with a favourite puppy

In this book, we aren't just lectured to about nature, we're taught to love and connect with it – through beautiful illustrations and a tone that's encouraging, warm and easy for children, and their favourite adults, to relate to.

ISBN: 978-1-912891-31-3

£15 | $19.99

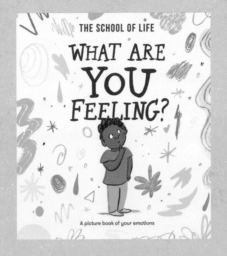

What Are You Feeling?

A picture book of your emotions

An illustrated guide helping children to identify and articulate how they are really feeling.

Feelings can be complicated to understand and difficult to explain. This book helps children to recognise their emotions and to find the right words to describe them. It encourages them to share their feelings in order to understand them and to manage them.

With beautiful illustrations, this sensitive and engaging book is designed to support the early steps of self-discovery and to create special moments for the sharing of thoughts and feelings, questions and ideas.

ISBN: 978-1-915087-27-0

£15 | $19.99

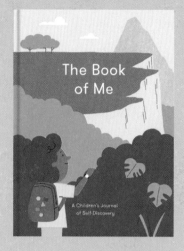

The Book of Me

A children's journal of self-discovery

An engaging guided journal for developing children's understanding of themselves and their emotions.

Children love to explore, born with a boundless desire to understand the world around them. While most of the outside world has already been mapped, there's a whole other world that has yet to be discovered, one that's accessible only to them: their own minds.

The Book of Me is a guided journal of self-discovery. It takes readers on a journey inside themselves, helping them explore their mind, their moods, their imagination, their conscience, and how they determine the course of their lives. Alongside wise and engaging explanations of ideas, each chapter contains a wealth of interactive exercises that together help to create a rich and unique self-portrait. Through writing, drawing, cutting out and colouring in, children can begin to untangle the mysteries of existence and work out who they really are (and who they might become...).

Combining psychology, philosophy and sheer fun, *The Book of Me* is an introduction to the vital art of self-knowledge, showing how it can help us grow into calmer, wiser and more rounded human beings.

ISBN: 978-1-912891-61-0

£18 | $24.99

Happy, Healthy Minds

A children's guide to emotional wellbeing

An essential guide to emotional wellbeing for children; tackling everyday issues to facilitate happier, healthier lives.

Our minds are beautifully complicated and brilliant machines. For much of our lives, these machines run efficiently with minimal maintenance. However, just like our other organs, they do require some proper attention every now and then and recognising this at an early age can only help as children progress into adulthood.

This is a guide designed to help children become more aware of their emotional needs and examines a range of topics that might give their minds difficulties, for example:

- when parents don't seem to understand us
- when we're finding it hard to make friends
- when school feels boring or difficult
- when we feel angry, or anxious, or lack confidence

There are atlases out there that describe the continents of the world. This book acts as an atlas to a child's mind, mapping out emotions and moods they may well have felt but not understood so clearly before.

We explore a range of common scenarios encountered by young children and talk about some of the very best ideas to help deal with them. By offering a sympathetic and supportive framework, *Happy, Healthy Minds* encourages children to open up, explore their own feelings and face the dilemmas of growing up armed with emotional intelligence.

ISBN: 978-1-912891-19-1

£18 | $24.99

Published in 2020 by The School of Life
First published in the USA in 2021
930 High Road, London, N12 9RT

This paperback edition published in 2023
Copyright © The School of Life 2020

Illustrations © Rachael Saunders

Designed and typeset by @marciamihotichstudio
Printed in China by Leo Paper Group

The School of Life publishes a range of books on essential
topics in psychological and emotional life, including
relationships, parenting, friendship, careers and fulfilment.
The aim is always to help us to understand ourselves better
– and thereby to grow calmer, less confused and more
purposeful. Discover our full range of titles, including books
for children, here: www.theschooloflife.com/books

 The School of Life also offers a comprehensive therapy
service, which complements, and draws upon, our published
works: www.theschooloflife.com/therapy

www.theschooloflife.com

ISBN 978-1-915087-19-5

10 9 8 7 6 5 4 3 2 1